Globalization
A Changing World

by Lisa Benjamin

Table of Contents

Millmark
EDUCATION

People around the world are alike and different.

These photographs show people in Moscow, Russia.

Talk about the photos.

What are the children doing?

The children are _____.

How does Moscow seem different from the place where you live?

Moscow seems different because _____.

Choose one activity in the photos. Tell how it is like something you do.

shoppers in downtown Moscow, Russia

RUSSIA

•Moscow

children in Moscow

tourists at St. Basil's Cathedral

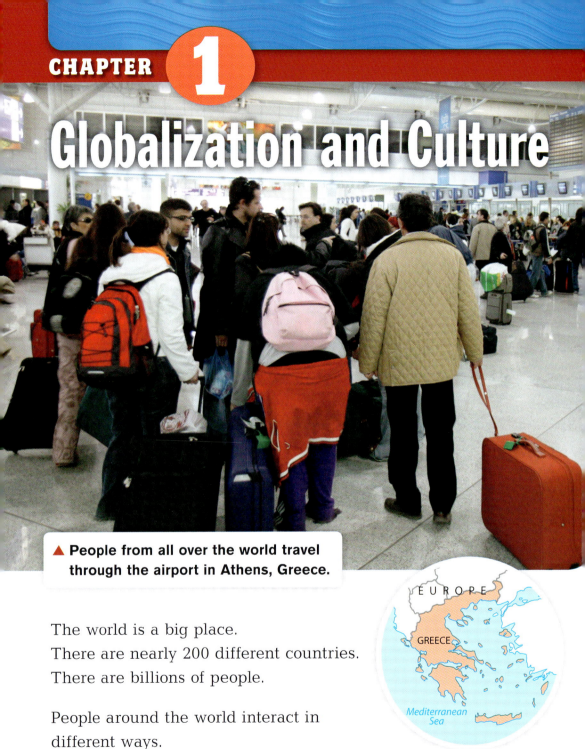

CHAPTER 1

Globalization and Culture

▲ **People from all over the world travel through the airport in Athens, Greece.**

The world is a big place.
There are nearly 200 different countries.
There are billions of people.

People around the world interact in
different ways.
When people interact, they can learn
about different **cultures**.

Culture is the way that people in one group live their lives.
Culture includes their beliefs, customs, art, and behaviors.
For example, many people visit Greece.
They learn about Greek culture.

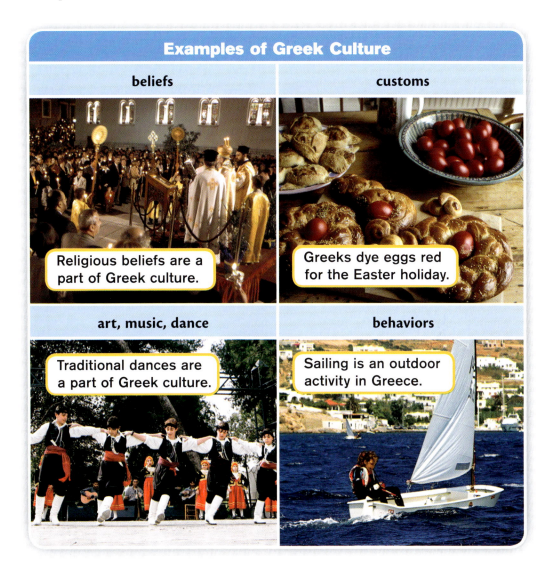

Examples of Greek Culture

beliefs

Religious beliefs are a part of Greek culture.

customs

Greeks dye eggs red for the Easter holiday.

art, music, dance

Traditional dances are a part of Greek culture.

behaviors

Sailing is an outdoor activity in Greece.

KEY IDEAS People around the world interact in different ways. When people interact, they can learn about other cultures.

Sometimes people interact through immigration.
When people immigrate, they come to live in a new country.
They bring their culture with them.
They also learn about the culture of their new home.

Dancers in California celebrate a Greek holiday.

Explore Language

immigrate = come to a new country
immigration = the act of immigrating
immigrant = a person who immigrates

Sometimes people in different countries work together.
They can talk on the phone.
They can send e-mails.
They can use Web cameras and other Internet tools.

Sometimes people buy goods from other countries.
They find these goods in stores.
For example, your shoes might come from another country.

▼ **Web cameras help people work together.**

▲ **These shoes were made in China.**

KEY IDEA People in different countries interact through immigration, working together, or buying goods from other countries.

People around the world interact more and more.
This is called **globalization**.
Globalization is the exchange of cultures, ideas,
and goods around the world.
Globalization is changing our world.

▼ Globalization includes sharing ideas
with people from different cultures.

Explore Language

Globalization and
globe both come from
the Latin word *globus*,
meaning "ball."

KEY IDEA Globalization
is the exchange of
cultures, ideas, and
goods around the world.

INTERPRET DATA

Many international travelers visit the United States (U.S.). The bar graph shows how many international travelers came to three U.S. airports. Discuss the information in the bar graph.

1. How many international travelers came to the Miami airport in 2004?

   About _____ travelers came to the Miami airport in 2004.

2. Which airport had more international travelers in 2004 than in 2000?

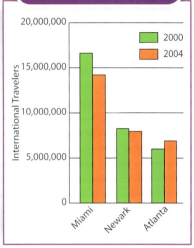

International Travelers in 2000 and 2004

SOURCE: U.S. Department of Transportation

MAKE CONNECTIONS

Culture includes the languages that people speak. What languages do you hear people speak? With a partner, make a list.

USE THE LANGUAGE OF SOCIAL STUDIES

What is culture?

Culture is the way that people in one group live their lives.

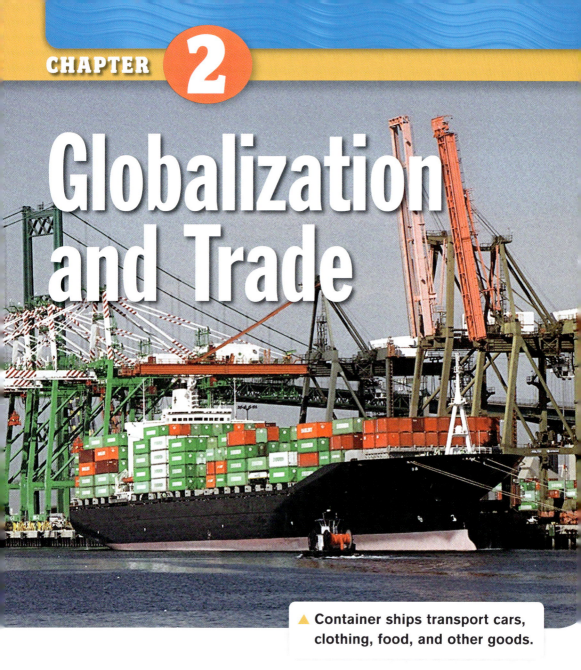

Globalization and Trade

▲ Container ships transport cars, clothing, food, and other goods.

Nations sell goods to other nations.
Nations buy goods from other nations.
The buying and selling of goods is called **trade**.
Nations interact through international trade.

Let's look at Canada and South Korea.
They interact through international trade.

In Canada, farmers grow wheat.
They grow more wheat than the people of Canada need.
So Canada sends the extra wheat to other nations.
In other words, Canada **exports** wheat.

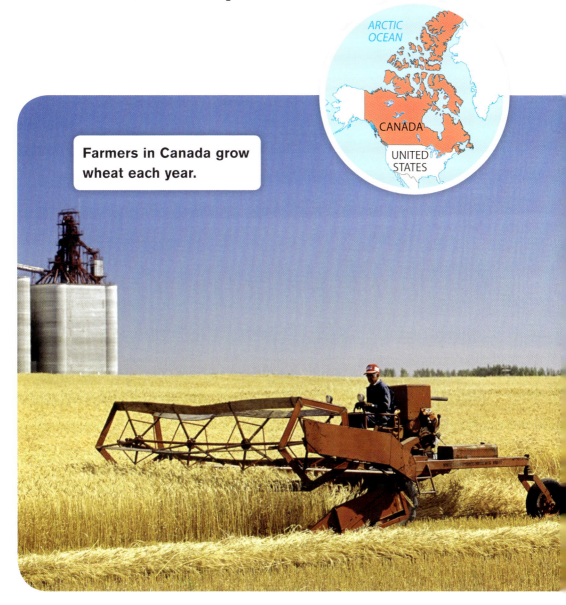

Farmers in Canada grow wheat each year.

South Korea needs more wheat.
So South Korea brings in wheat from Canada
and other nations.
In other words, South Korea **imports** wheat.

South Korean car companies make cars.
South Korea exports cars to Canada and
other nations.

▼ **South Korea exports cars to
Canada and other nations.**

International trade can help nations.
When a nation imports goods, people
can buy the things they want or need.
When a nation exports goods, the
nation can earn money.
There can be more jobs for people.

▲ Costa Rica exports coffee
beans. It imports cars.

▲ Like South Korea, Japan exports
cars. It imports coffee beans.

KEY IDEAS Nations
import goods they
want or need. Nations
export goods to earn
money.

Today, there is more international trade between nations.
Nations import more goods from other nations.
Nations export more goods to other nations.

Trade brings people from different cultures together.
International trade is an important part of globalization.

People from different cultures interact through international trade.

ASEAN-EU COMMEMORATIVE
22 NOVEMBER 2007

KEY IDEAS People and nations interact through international trade. International trade is an important part of globalization.

ANALYZE CAUSE AND EFFECT

Think about the causes and effects of effects of international trade. Make a graphic organizer like this one. Fill in the effects for each cause. Then share your ideas with a partner.

Cause	Effect
Canada grows more wheat than it needs.	Canada exports wheat to other countries.
South Korea does not grow enough wheat.	_____
Most countries don't make everything they need.	_____

MAKE CONNECTIONS

Many countries export clothing. Where are your clothes made? Look at the tags on your clothes. Make a list of the countries. With a partner, find the countries on a world map.

 STRATEGY FOCUS

Make Inferences

South Korea exports cars to Canada. What could happen if Canada starts to make more cars? What could happen to South Korea's exports? Make an inference.

Chapter 2: Globalization and Trade   **15**

Globalization and Technology

Globalization is not new.

People have always learned from other cultures.

People have always traveled from one place to another.

People have always traded goods.

More than 2,000 years ago, traders brought silk, spices, and other goods from China to Rome. It took years for the goods to reach Rome.

Today, new **technology** is changing the ways that people and nations interact. Technology is changing **communication**. For example, cell phones and computers help us communicate faster than before.

Technology is also changing **transportation**. Planes, ships, trains, and trucks are faster today than before.

▼ Planes are a fast form of transportation. It takes only ten hours to fly from Beijing, China, to Rome, Italy.

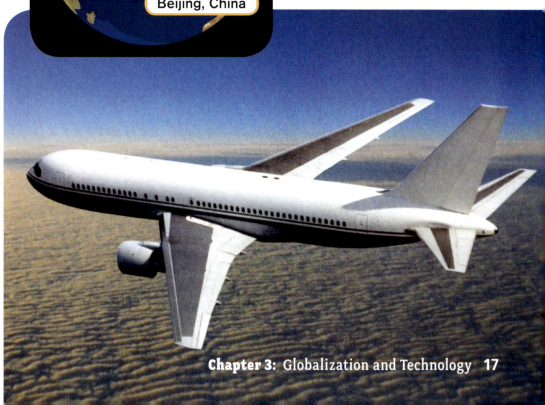

People can travel more easily now.

Goods are transported more quickly than before.

Communication is faster.

Nations interact more.

Globalization is happening faster than ever before.

▶ **Trains are faster than before.**

◀ **New technology has made communication faster.**

KEY IDEA

Changes in transportation and communication are speeding up globalization.

READ MAPS

Companies in Turkey export jeans. The map shows some countries that import jeans from Turkey. Use the map to answer the questions.

Importing Jeans

countries that import jeans

GERMANY   RUSSIA
UNITED STATES   ITALY   TURKEY

1. What are some countries that import jeans from Turkey?

   Some countries that import jeans from Turkey are _____.

2. Which of these countries is closest to Turkey?

3. Which country cannot receive the jeans by truck or train? Explain.

MAKE CONNECTIONS

Technology changes the ways we can communicate. How do you think we will communicate in the future? Draw a picture. Talk or write about your picture.

EXPAND VOCABULARY

Cars and airplanes are forms of **transportation**. What other forms of transportation can you name? Make a list. Include forms of transportation from long ago and today. Discuss your list with a partner.

Chapter 3: Globalization and Technology **19**

Importing and Exporting

International trade creates many different kinds of jobs. Here are a few examples. Find out more about these careers.

Workers	What They Do
dock workers	load and unload goods
inspectors	check goods before the goods enter a country
international bankers	help companies do business around the world

▲ Dock workers load and unload goods from ships.

▲ Inspectors make sure goods are safe to use and in good condition.

◄ International bankers make sure money moves from one country to another.

Statements and Examples

Sometimes a sentence states an idea. Then the next sentence gives an example that explains the idea. **For example** and **such as** are phrases that show examples.

EXAMPLES

Culture includes different forms of art. **For example**, culture includes music, dance, and theater.

Talk About It

Look through this book with a partner. State your ideas about international trade. Give examples to explain your ideas.

Write with Examples

Choose a Key Idea from this book. Then give examples.

- State the Key Idea in your own words.

- Give examples that explain the Key Idea.

Words You Can Use
for example such as

Many Countries, One Pair of Jeans

Sometimes one good is made by people working in different countries. Look at the flowchart. It shows one example of how this can happen.

1 In China, farmers grow cotton.

2 In India, workers use the cotton to make cloth.

3 In Mexico, workers sew the cloth into jeans.

1. Explain what happens first, next, and finally.

First, _____.   Next, _____.

Finally, _____.

2. How do you think the cloth is transported from India to Mexico?

communication an exchange of information
Computers can make **communication** faster.

culture (cultures) the way that people in one group live their lives
This kind of dance is a part of Greek **culture**.

globalization the exchange of cultures, ideas, and goods around the world
Globalization includes sharing ideas with people from different cultures.

technology the use of scientific knowledge to solve problems or make something easier
Technology has changed the way we communicate.

trade the exchange of goods
Container ships allow more **trade** between nations.

transportation a way of moving people or goods
Trains are used for the **transportation** of goods.

Index

MILLMARK EDUCATION CORPORATION
Ericka Markman, President and CEO; Karen Peratt, VP, Editorial Director; Lisa Bingen, VP, Marketing; Dave Willette, VP, Sales; Rachel L. Moir, VP, Operations and Production; Shelby Alinsky, Associate Editor; Janet Battiste, Language Editor; Pictures Unlimited, Photo Research; Arleen Nakama, Technology Projects

PROGRAM AUTHORS
Mary Hawley, Program Author, Instructional Design
Peggy Altoff, Program Author, Social Studies

STUDENT BOOK DEVELOPMENT
Gare Thompson Associates, Inc.

BOOK DESIGN
Dinardo Design LLC

TECHNOLOGY
Six Red Marbles

CONTENT REVIEWER
Margit McGuire, PhD, Program Director and Professor of Teacher Education, Seattle University, Seattle, WA

PROGRAM ADVISORS
Scott K. Baker, PhD, Pacific Institutes for Research, Eugene, OR
Carla C. Johnson, EdD, University of Toledo, Toledo, OH
Margit McGuire, PhD, Seattle University, Seattle, WA
Donna Ogle, EdD, National-Louis University, Chicago, IL
Betty Ansin Smallwood, PhD, Center for Applied Linguistics, Washington, DC
Gail Thompson, PhD, Claremont Graduate University, Claremont, CA
Emma Violand-Sánchez, EdD, Arlington Public Schools, Arlington, VA (retired)

PHOTO CREDITS Cover ©Jonny Le Fortune/zefa/Corbis; IFC and 15a ©David Safanda/iStockphoto.com; 1a ©Arvind Balaraman/Shutterstock; 2a, 4b, 9c, 11b, 12b, 13a, 13b, 19a, 22a Mapping Specialists; 2-3a and 3b ©Gonzalo Azumendi/age fotostock; 3a ©Les Stone/Sygma/Corbis; 4a ©Vario images Gmbh & Co.KG/Alamy; 5a ©Hapsis/IML/age fotostock; 5b ©Fresh Food Images/Photolibrary; 5c and 5d ©Sami Moudavaris/Alamy; 6a and 23b ©Kayte Deioma/Photo Edit; 7a ©Robert Llewellyn/age fotostock; 7b ©Ronen/Shutterstock; 8a, 20c, 23c ©Michael Newman/Photo Edit; 8b ©Morgan Lane Photography/Shutterstock; 9a and 9b Photos by Ken Karp; 10a and 23e ©AP Images/Rene Macura; 11a ©Mike Grandmaison/age fotostock; 12a ©Ho New/REUTERS; 13c ©AP Images/Koji Sasahara; 13d ©ARCO/W Layer/age fotostock; 14a ©AP Images/Romeo Gacad; 16a ©Gavin Hellier/Alamy; 17a and 23d ©Flirt Collection/Photolibrary; 17b ©AP Images; 17c ©Tom Van Sant/Geosphere Project, Santa Monica/Photo Researchers, Inc.; 18a ©David Noton Photography/Alamy; 18b ©Russell Kord/Alamy; 19b ©Feng Yu; 20a ©Jim West/Alamy; 20b ©AP Images/Jean-marc Bouju; 21a ©Anyka/Shutterstock; 22a ©Mapping Specialists; 22b ©Antonio D'Albore/age fotostock; 22c ©Indiapicture/Alamy; 22d ©Reuters/Jennifer Szymaszek; 23a ©David Young-Wolff/Photo Edit; 23f ©Heeb Christian/age fotostock; 24a ©Losevsky Pavel

Published by Millmark Education Corporation
PO Box 30239
Bethesda, MD 20824

ISBN-13: 978-1-4334-0672-0

Printed in the USA

10 9 8 7 6 5 4 3 2 1